GATEWAY
TO
OBSCURITY

Life in Verse

May you hour of
enlighteament
KW

KEN WESTDORP

ARCHWAY
PUBLISHING

Archway Publishing books may be ordered through booksellers or by contacting:

Archway Publishing
1663 Liberty Drive
Bloomington, IN 47403
www.archwaypublishing.com
1 (888) 242-5904

ISBN: 978-1-4808-4549-7 (sc)
ISBN: 978-1-4808-4550-3 (hc)
ISBN: 978-1-4808-4551-0 (e)

Library of Congress Control Number: 2017906951

Print information available on the last page.

Archway Publishing rev. date: 5/10/2017

THE GATE

Flourishing dandelions
worship the faded
white, wooden
picket gate.

Stranded castoff,
obsolete and abandoned,
sorely neglected
by society.

Nostalgically designed
with practical purpose;
denied repair,
instead replaced.

Momentary scene
whispers a story,
opened opportunity
into unknown.

Imaginary route
where possibilities exist,
distorted wonders
beyond reality.

A Mother's Love

I thank you so much
for bringing me forth in life,
nurturing me through gestation,
ensuring my eventual birth.

In childhood, I suckled your breasts,
gaining strength and further development.
Within your arms, I found love
and comfort from loneliness.

You taught me understanding
and encouraged my dreams.
When I was ill or injured,
you aided in my recovery.

During times of family squabbling,
you sheltered me from the storm.
Acting on my behalf,
you helped keep the family intact.

At times I would abuse your love,
subjecting it to teenage rage,
the terrible names I called you
torturing you in awful ways.

How fortunate to have you as a mother,
with all the trouble I've put you through.
I know I don't say it often enough,
but you're my best friend in the world.

THE OLD HOMESTEAD

Though long ago replaced
by several new developments,
the place I was born
will never be forgotten.

A modest, one-story structure,
never meant for a growing family.

Living-room fireplaces
often heated the home.
Backyard gardens
were a necessity of life.

Back then, neighbours
were considered friends,
and grandparents
lived just next door.

As children, we ventured
down nearby streets,

engaging our imagination
instead of playing electronics.

Overcrowded malls,
like Guildford
and Surrey Place,
were far-off places.

Instead, we frequented
neighbourhood shops.

Libraries were smaller
and crowded with books.

Childhood playtime
and holiday gatherings
were documented
in black-and-white movies.
Aging photographs
preserve fond memories
of my parents
and our family.

Many familiar features
have all disappeared.

As for the old homestead
on 132nd Street near 72nd Avenue,
many random dwellings
now occupy the space.

STEPS

Cautious fumbling
upon unknown terrain.
Stumbling strides
inch farther along.

Childhood foolishness
breaks new ground,
monumental challenges
conquered without hesitation.

Restrictions enforced
limit bounds of exploration.
Instructional guidance
forces individual compliance.

Government controls
seize political protests,
commercial enterprises
monopolized by a few.

Spirits dwindle;
compliance takes hold.

FATHER AND SON

When life's incidentals
come to a screeching halt,
burdened by complications,
the result of neglected health,
miracles of medicine
prevent ultimate disaster.
However, reckless behaviour
necessitates lengthy recovery.
Incapacitated by weakness,
reduced to an invalid,
struggling with adversities
taken previously for granted.
Minor physical accomplishments
account as major achievements,
proving that a person's measure
is the legacy one leaves behind.

PRETEEN ANGST

No longer a boy,
yet to be a man.
Caught between two worlds,
struggling to understand.

Preteen angst—
life's greatest mystery.

Confused as to where
and why things are happening.
Cursed by nature
and traumatic changes.

Endless wandering
in a sea of entanglement.

Preteen angst,
subject of consequence.

Struggling with the loss
of youth and innocence.
Searching for the truth
to lasting identity.

Overcome by influence,
trying to fit in.
Rebelling against parents
and the guidance they give.

Driven by independence
while shackled by control.
A slave to increasing reality,
whose master is unrelenting.

Preteen angst,
a ritual of dances.

Overwhelmed by demands
and social responsibilities.
A piece within the puzzle,
prisoner to the illusion.

In the midst of danger,
the questions seem too great.
Plagued by confusion,
there seems no promise of escape.

Preteen angst,
opportunity requires certain risks.

WEAK

Strength and bravery
fractured by humanity.
Understanding beneath
a hardened shell.

Weak, yet courageous
to demonstrate emotions.

Bold and unafraid
of lurking darkness.
Vulnerable to attachments,
tugging at the heart.

Legendary heroics
and physical bravado.

Conscious objectors
who negotiate peace.

A powerful warrior,
ready to do battle.
Defender of innocents
with little regard to self.

Dedicated soldier
to a justified cause.
Defiant and righteous
in protecting the sacred.

Steadfast commitment
beneath human fragility.
A true believer
grounded by compassion.

Resilient to adversity,
grounded by understanding.

Riddled by imperfections,
empowered with salvation.

Mere mortal heroes,
challenging insurmountable odds.
Champions of the oppressed,
taking a stand.

Ordinary people
making the ultimate sacrifice.

CHILDHOOD MENTOR

Farewell,
gentle soul
who nurtured generations.
A childhood mentor
who instilled
love.

Despite political
and civil unrest,
you remained true.

Among the neighbourhood
were such memorable characters
as Speedy Delivery and King Friday,
to name but a few.

Without fail,
you were there.

Mr. Rogers.

Less sophisticated
than his contemporaries.

Loved by all,
the boys and girls
who tuned in to
his morning show.

A welcoming smile
with a gentle voice
of absolute warmth.

Beyond,
there awaits
a magical place.
Though now gone,
your influence will
remain.

FAMILY DYNAMICS

Brothers and sisters,
aunts and uncles,
cousins, nephews, and nieces
form an extended family
united by blood
or through marriage.

Long-ago mistakes
become outstanding grudges
that shake the foundation.

Childish errors
blown out of proportion,
solation of innocents,
guilt by association.

Immature behaviour
exaggerates the situation.

Family dynamics

once built upon
a structure of love.

Elements of survival
dictate the necessity
of overall cooperation
and ability to forgive.

Lessons from the past
mustn't interfere with
establishing a future.

Unity and understanding,
respect and trust,
honesty, forgiveness, and love
must prevail over
petty grievances
that wedge a family apart.

MIDDLE CHILD

Neither beginning
nor end, but in the middle.
Fighting for identity
among sibling rivalry.

Often overlooked
is the middle child.

Burdened with the yoke
of the eldest sibling.
Neglected by parents
who pampered the baby.

Struggling for attention
with disastrous results.
Living within a fantasy
in order to be appreciated.

Growing isolation
leads to greater rebellion.

A middle-syndrome,
troublesome child.

Exhibiting behaviour
of radical nature.
A growing nuisance
to a perfect family.

Revealing emotions
with artistic flair.

Labelled childish
and typical of middle born.

Perseverance overcomes
artificial expectation.
Newly recognized creativity
gradually becomes appreciated.

Eventually, balance
adds some stability.
Maturity and understanding
heal earlier conflicts.

Growing admiration
for the middle child.

Situated at the centre
by virtue of birth,
meaning found within
a child's search for purpose.

INVISIBLE

Hidden within conformity,
labelled with an identity
instituted by society.
Afraid of possibilities
that challenge one's ability
within a harsh reality.

One among
the masses,
isolated and alone.

Striving to achieve
what others conceive.
Struggling with beliefs
fabricated by deceit.

Abandoned by
Trusted allies ...

Invisible.

Cherished for
establishing a voice.

Gaining a foothold
overtop the old.
Achieving a bold
presence beyond the fold.

Individual stamina
from necessity
and determination.

Camouflaged behind secrecy
and highly valued privacy,
brings forth a legacy.
Steadfast transparency
evokes greater certainty
in one's advocacy.

SPONTANEITY

Childhood innocence
and abandoned responsibility,
limitless imagination
of incredible possibility.

Chaotic movement
inspired by delirium.

Unhesitant reactions
to difficult situations;
profound inspiration
in artistic creation.

Naive exploration
of taboo subjects,
unusual perspective
to delicate situations.

Adrenalin rush
sparks greater achievement.

Daredevil acrobatics
widen personal perspective.

Amateur,
developed opportunity
suggests differing possibilities
without considering ramifications,

impeding progressive
reality.

Enthusiastic gestures
cause chain reactions.

Charismatic demonstrations
build further momentum.

Uninhibited genius
and further determination
persuade pessimism
into a positive attitude.

Wild splendour,
unleashed from captivity,
spiritual enlightenment
finally awakened.

Spontaneous motion
elicits surprise reactions.

Improvised characteristics
embellish the illusion
that ultimately motivates
a mental conviction.

SINGULARITY

Singularity ...

An anomaly
among the universe.

Caught within
a hostile territory,
where one exists
without a purpose.

Gradually gaining
a foothold
of awareness.

Establishing a
foundation in a place
constantly bombarded by chaos.
Searching for an ally
who will share
a relationship.

Incremental momentum
causes success
to overwhelm failure.

Exploring realms
well beyond self,
when two become
integrated within society.

An extension
of humanity.

Pluralism ...

UNSUSPECTING REALITY

Life's monumental junctures
overwhelm my physical stability.
Stamina and agility
add consequence to mortality.

Unsuspecting reality
judges me as obsolete.

A child of yesterday,
struggling in today's world
of technological adversity
and cultural upheaval.

Forced into exile
by a generational gap.
An out-of-touch geriatric
prescribed assorted medication.

Hospital visits
render complicated issues.
Unsuspecting reality
diagnoses me as pessimistic.

Bygone years
etch symptoms of dementia.
Memory lapses
indicate growing signs of Alzheimer's.

Alterations in characteristics
inflict physical abnormalities.
Changes in lifestyle
inhibit thoughts of recklessness.

Unsuspecting reality
causes lengthy reflection.

Burden by regrets
of errors in the past.
Endowed with wisdom
from a multitude of mistakes.

TOWARD MANHOOD

Human qualities
I deservedly lack:
responsibility,
strength,
humanity,
and respect.

Important aspects
I often overlook:
understanding,
forgiveness,
love,
and wisdom.

Evolutionary stages
I carelessly wasted:
compassion,
depth,
insight,
and maturity.

None of which
can be bought,
nor necessarily
acquired with age.

Often intelligence
overwhelms the situation.

Instead, experience
proves a better teacher.

Careful reflection
allows further growth,
the ability to listen
to one's inner voice.

Achievements that make
a boy into a man.

Caught between Two Places

Freedom
and responsibility
confuse the life
once my own.

Age
and maturity
override the desires
I once had.

Daring
and insight
challenge the ability
to stand alone.

Individuals in partnership,
struggling
against the inevitable
sacrifice.

Instruments of passion,
reluctantly
dealing with love's
complexity.

Innocents from persuasion
overwhelmingly
influenced by outside
forces.

Caught
between two places,
one
must realize the consequences.

A Glimpse of Fatherhood

An opportunity
naturally denied,
yet included by
another's generosity.

Children drawn
to my immaturity.

Playful moments
of eager foolishness.
Displays of imagination
not burdened by responsibility.

Temporary distraction
alleviates a mother's guilt.
Overwhelming pressures
of a single parent.

Attentive to the needs
of a developing mind.

Glimpses of fatherhood,
utilizing spontaneous talent.

Enriching a mind
with trivial facts
and engaging tricks.
Building a foundation

for academic learning
in a scientific realm.

Minimizing dangers
in a chaotic world.

Ensuring safety
of a loved one.

Burden with separation
from external forces.
Ignoring a lover
over a child's needs.

Troubled by a
faltering relationship.
Changing directions
while hurting an innocent.

Drowning in confusion
over unforeseen circumstance.

Unsure of my place
observing from afar
the child I fostered.

REFLECTIONS

Life's accumulation
segmented
by split-second
decisions.

Youthful recklessness
hurts innocent people.

Rippled images
fracture
the intended
perfection.

Mischievous exploits
devoid of consciousness.

Complete carelessness
toward future endeavours.

Desperate measures
overshadow
the achievement
of success.

Deafening echoes
pursue
an inescapable
judgment.

Defying authority
with absolute contempt.

Ignoring caution,
overlooking the obvious.

Rambling lyrics
compel
a mob
mentality.

Embedded hostility
ignites an inferno.

Shifting currents
necessitate
a mortal
reflection.

GUILTY PLEASURES

Sweet,
indulgent weaknesses
exploit
tender mercies.

Perverted
physical stimulants
inflict
latten guilt.

Devilishly
wicked influence
undermines
sincere commitments.

Excessive
consumer consummation
ignores
inevitable consequences.

Reckless
disregard of thought,
searching
elusive promise.

Hurdling
toward destruction,
salvation
becomes abandoned.

Predators
challenge existence,
neglecting
self-preservation.

Mesmerized,
manipulated innocents,
tempted
forbidden fruit.

Purpose
suddenly obscured,
commitment
promises hope.

1-2 MANY SORRIES

My melodramatic episodes
earlier concealed
behind a romantic facade.

An act of desperation
from a lonely soul.

My immature behaviour,
once thought cute,
now fuels your frustration.

A troubled childhood
I have never fully escaped.

Foolishness and
false bravado
I wear like armour
to hide my vulnerability.

A man without a purpose,
searching for answers.

Your constant badgering
enrages the beast
that I have become.

A struggle from someone
who's battered by self-doubt.

Friends and family
question the validity
of a peculiar relationship.

Sorries flow like water,
yet understanding remains elusive.

Our stubborn convictions
impede the success of
communication.

DECEPTION

Ridiculed and confused
as to life's designated role.
Subjected to expectations
far beyond anyone's control.

Engaging in a fantasy
while concealing vulnerability.
Manipulator of circumstance,
searching for escape
from the vast unknown.

Loss of personal identity
makes coping with reality
that much easier than before.

A master of all deception
often fools oneself.

ANTICIPATION

I never accepted
that you'd leave,
though your departure
was planned in advance.

I felt empty
even though we tried
to keep in touch.

Text messages
and Internet e-mails
were of little consolation
to the pain I felt inside.

Everywhere I looked,
I was constantly
reminded of you.

Work became a temporary
means of distraction
while evenings and weekends
were occupied by reflection.

Each day
meant one day closer
to your return.

Weeks apart
turned into desperation
as I contemplated
reckless thoughts.

My only salvation
was the promise
of our physical passion.

Any troubles
that threatened our romance
now seem trivial
against the far greater picture.
A promising future
so long as we're committed
to making it last.

SECRETS

Convenient omissions
of a factual nature.
Overlooked details
misplace precise answers.

Unpleasant matters
hidden by denial.

Delicate embellishments
pacify a sensitive situation.
Verbal obscurity
avoids hostile confrontation.

Yesterday's digressions
shrouded within time.

Personal opinions
told in strict confidence.
Disturbing memories
tempered with half-truths.

Confidential burdens
troubled by guilt.

Negligent acts
made out of unfortunates.
Little secrets
reinforce the hollow believes.

CONFESSION

Beneath
a thinly veiled façade
hides a momentary error,
complications that add to
a lifetime of
regrets.

Sadness and anger
greet my final
admission-

something
that should have been
forthcoming so very
long ago.

Opportunity for honesty
often presented itself.

Confessions

I might have
admitted instead of deceit.

Trust
between two people
severely damaged beyond
repair.

A lifetime
of lengthy reflection
seems justified.

Perhaps
I might regain
your devotion and respect.
Commitment and loyalty
is, after all, what
you deserve.

CONSEQUENCE

Cause and effect
accumulated learning experience.
A multitude of repercussions
to human interactions.
Errors in judgment
complicate physical impairment.

Turmoil of emotions
spark a turbulent commotion
among those of certain devotion.

Amateur curiosity
induced by thoughts of notoriety.
Bullied by society
complicates feelings of anxiety.

Risky behaviour
enhances a negative
consequence.

Magnify insecurity
behind historical failure.

Studied variety
motivates ideas of rivalry.
Mocked by naivety,
subjected to thoughts of vanity.

Cast upon the ocean,
awash in twirling motion,
surrounded by hostile corruption.

Brief thoughts of enhancement
require last-minute adjustment.
Instinctive human reaction
tampered by artificial distraction.
Amassed human knowledge
and calculated risk.

ISOLATION

Caught within
an emotional storm,
challenged and conflicted
by bouts of confusion.

Abandoned by the human race,
a casualty out of place.

Bounced from responsibility,
medicated on pharmaceuticals,
ensured a lifestyle
of endless addiction.

Isolation from humanity
offers a margin of salvation.

A product of obsolete technology
relegated to the past.
No greater significance
than a government static.

Labelled an anarchist,
a terrorist, and anti-establishment.
Attacked and persecuted,
convicted without having committed a crime.

Captive to uncertainty,
manifested by demons and illusions.

A hostage to the evil
inflicted by figures of trust.

Tempted by suicide,
induced by hostile forces.
Authorities that victimize
the multitude of innocent.

Clinging to reality,
my life slips through
reflections cast by
brittle fingertips.

Perhaps beyond,
there exists fulfilment
I was denied while on earth.

DRIFTING

Slipping
into illusion
while anchored in reality.

Cast
upon waves
that lap over emotions.

Propelled
by forces
of chaos without end.

Spiralling
out of control,
down empty corridors.

Worlds collide
into a malaise
of shadow and light.

Limitless perception
infects mental stability
and delicate equilibrium.

Physical paralysis
impedes basic function
beyond one's will.

An indecisive struggle
more, more difficult to fight.

Released from responsibility,
temptations increasingly overwhelm.

Portals into another realm
offer chances of greater insight.

Parental Expectations

Conflicts
and a lack of consultation
alienate each generation,
guilt and manipulation
upholding productivity,
managing the family business.

Artistic merit
belittled as frivolous
and childish.

Abandoned dreams
inflict teenage regret.
Necessary responsibilities
overshadow another's pursuits.

Unspoken regrets
enforce a stringent agenda.

Parental expectations
ignite rifts
between family members.

Academic challenges
to an imaginative mind.
Rules and regulations
over creativity.

Talented behaviour
squandered beneath
a father's ambitions.

Hardship and anger
drive a wedge between
father and son.
Time and reflection
help to overcome,
sever roadblocks.

A Fork in the Road

Everyday decisions
often complicated by
unknown conclusions.
Random choices
with built-in dangers
and unforeseen consequences.

Endless formalities
develop out of simplicity
found in daily life.

Life's ultimate outcome
is determined by
the fork
in the road.

Crossing over
from one moment
to the next.
Gambling survival
on the suggestion
of a hunch.

Lured by deception
and momentary gain
leads to a great
deal of pain.

The fork in the road
has no preconceived notion
as to what the future holds.

Standing at the crossroads,
life will only pass you by.

Venture down the highway,
where U-turns are forbidden
and the route is littered
with endless detours.

CATASTROPHIC CIRCUMSTANCE

Foreboding clouds gather
before the impending storm.
Shadows dance across
my bedroom walls.

Parents impose reality,
rob me of any creativity
with a zealous sense of security.

Am I destined for a life of obscurity?

Gritty images materialize
from childhood illusions.
Monsters stir within
cautionary folklore.

Darkened rituals incite
forces lurking from beyond,
spirits hovering over
those who tempt fate.

Teachers enforce authority,
dictate the absurdity
of attempted spontaneity.

Have good intentions
all but abandoned me?

Silenced by those
who would prosecute
and incarcerate me.
Why am I relentlessly victimized?

Does anyone acknowledge
my sorrowful pleas?
Am I just another captive
of a capitalist society?

Government-sanctioned morality
authorizes the necessity
of torture and brutality.
Where is the sense
of possible tranquillity?

Drained of all emotions,
I resurrect my will.
Vengeance is a certainty;
so God has prophesized.

Basking in self-righteousness,
angels shall conquer hostility,
vanquishing all false deities.

Does there exist a better plan?

Nevermore shall mankind
orchestrate global atrocities.
Greed and hatred should never
corrupt an everlasting love.

With patience and understanding,
any difference can be reconciled.
Bring about harmony
within nature's garden.

Generations have squandered
countless opportunities,
ignored predicted warnings.

Perhaps overall consideration
should revaluate the plan?

Mounting consequences
ensure our extinction.
Nature will evolve,
devoid of man's role.

None shall dominate the earth;
instead, all species will operate
in the other's best interest.

So shall it be,
lest we change?

MISTAKES

Thoughtless errors
and unfortunate circumstance.

Careless misjudgements
and difficult consequences.

Foolish endeavours
and reckless conclusions.

Human frailty,
emotional turmoil,
cause and effect.

Childish behaviour,
physical athletics,
actions and results.

Moral dilemmas,
mental lapse,
situation and solution.

Insightful reflections
garnered
over time.

Unexpected mistakes—
life's
greatest lessons.

MIDLIFE CRISIS

Gray hairs
hold no silver lining.
Wiry whiskers
sprout from nose and ears.

Youthful years behind me,
I got the
midlife crisis blues.

Substantial gain
physically impairs me.
Decreased mobility
from lack of energy.

Daredevil antics just a memory
to man who suffers
the midlife crisis blues.

Sexual disinterest
adds major turmoil.
Prescription drugs
help medicate the problem.

Longevity quickly dwindles
for someone condemned
to the midlife crisis blues.

Passion
and spontaneity
have all but
abandoned me.

Sentenced forever
to a midlife crisis
blues.

Sickness
and death
seem to offer
ultimate escape.

CLARITY

A multitude of niceties often confuse the means of under-
standing what it is a person says. Political correctness shields
one from causing damage should true opinions be made
clear. Round and round the conversation travels, with few
answers to the problems that plague us on a daily basis. Self-
preservation seems the order of the day in a campaign filled
with gestures and very little substance.

Honesty is often painful to those who refuse to compromise
on matters that are embedded within the heart. Matters that
have passion and loyalty to tradition often impede the road
that leads to progress.

Often the simplest of disagreements can manifest into feuds
that last for years and years, dividing later generations.
Mistakes are as much a part of the human condition as are
love and sadness, and yet pursuit toward perfection puts
limits on human development. Just as a diamond's value is
based upon its flaws, so should we embrace our imperfec-
tions as gifts from above.

With an open heart and ears to hear the road toward greater
understanding of human nature can be shared with others.
The foundation of compromise has more to do with give
and take than any short-term victory celebration. To accom-
plish this, there must be absolute clarity.

EXILES

Tempers flare,
volatile rifts.

Forces isolation,
dramatic consolation.

Scarred
from within
by thoughtless
action.

Lonely exiles
craving another.

Silent reflection
decides selection.

Awkward
senses interpret
a fragile
balance.

Passion erupts
biological instinct.

Love or lust?

LIMITATIONS

Bound by definitions
established long ago.

Prisoner to my ailments
I find increasingly
difficult to ignore.
Confronted by challenges
that seem insurmountable
to my escape.

Limited by abilities
instituted through force
and acts of secrecy.

Tangled among weeds,
weakness becomes apparent
to those in power.
Questions overwhelm answers
in a struggle to find clarity,
lost in the eternal storm.

Surrounded and frightened,
doubt becomes magnified
by the unknown.

Overwhelmed with uncertainty
toward the meaning
behind existence.

Alone against the elements,
fighting for survival
despite the inevitable.

A moment within
the endless span of time.

CURIOUS FLIRTATIONS

Lingering glances
toward the opposite sex.

Sexual arousal
elicit my temptation.

Moments of
imaginative possibilities
curtailed by a
lengthy relationship.

Innuendo conversations
spark underlying passion.

Physical assistance
leaves a lasting impression.

Memorable scent
stirs up wild fascination.

Opportunities with
insurmountable consequence
cause emotional turmoil.

Intriguing personality
stimulates further investigation.

Friendly conversation
ignites previous stagnation.

Challenges
overwhelm responsibility
existent upon
will and desire.

WANTS AND DESIRES

Obligations and objections
gather in resentment.

Demands and commitments
change into opposition.

Responsibilities and promises
become one's deterrent.

Awareness and maturity
expected in adulthood.
Distant childish antics
animate spontaneous behaviour.

Greed and necessity
impose unbearable restriction.
Heightened volatile conflicts
endanger future opportunities.

Compromise and compassion
sacrificed by wants.
Love and understanding
isolated from desire.

Passionate entanglements
perceived as neglect.

Altered perceptions
alienate the past.

Emotional recovery
erased by pain.

Ignorant offspring
incarcerate the self.

STARRY EYED LOVERS

You fulfil
my heart's every desire.

Like starry-eyed lovers
whose hopes and ambitions
are manifested in dreams.
Navigating between daily routines
toward new frontiers
of emotional adventure.

The love we share
is as vast
as the universe.

Exhilarated by the mysteries
of uncharted and hostile
territory of the human anatomy.
Searching for the ultimate
climactic physical reaction
to solidify a connection.

The vows we exchange
are as true
as our devotion.

Cast within strident roles
embedded in tradition and rules
we struggle to escape.

Restless from conformity,
tempted by chance
of an elusive future.

Together united
against a solitary tide.

THE OTHER MAN

Beneath a web of secrecy:
hidden,
veiled,
and concealed,
someone else exists.

Cast within a shadow:
qualities,
memories,
and abilities
seemingly beyond belief.

Made from purest sympathy:
judgement,
comparisons,
and reflections
based upon embellishment.

Written out of importance:
humbled,
confused,
and frustrated,
emotional injury transpires.

How does another
become part of the establishment?

Why must tragedy
jeopardize love's renewed success?

What will change
achieve that time has eluded?

Where can progress
succeed a future thought abandoned?

And when
does tomorrow begin?

DISTANCE BETWEEN US

Off
you have flown
to a faraway land.

Your imminent departure
seemed like an eternity.

All
I ever wanted
was to hold your hand.

But emotional consequence
led us in separate ways.

Foolishly,
my thoughts of insecurity
manifested into immaturity.

Conflicts of responsibility
provided my easy escape.

Alone
to contemplate
yet another heartbreak.

Stranded in darkness,
I realize my mistakes.

Tomorrow
will eventually
bring you back.

Change will certainly
alter our relationship.

Reunited
by necessity,
our future awaits.

From that day forward,
fate has made a plan.

Empty Promises

Vows
between lovers:
honour,
respect,
and loyalty.

Pledges
unifying souls:
understanding,
communication,
and honesty.

Oaths
entwine feelings:
desires,
compassion,
and fulfilment.

None of these promises
last for very
long.

Temporary difficulties
gain greater
complexity.

Little incidents
develop further
imbalance.

Simple arguments
instigate a vicious
war.

Empty promises
meaningless without
substance.

WHISPERS

Deep reflection of pent-up emotions
suppressed by a moral majority.
Expressions of inner creativity
demonized by others,
fragmented into
whispers
verbalizing images,
defying hardened rational.
Ideas of far-reaching implications
riddled with opinion of radical thoughts.

LOVERS ... NOW FRIENDS

Thoughts of lustful satisfaction
drown righteous moral code,
neglecting adult responsibility
for a momentary pleasure.

Manipulating sexual desires
in a game of chance.
Hoping for an opportunity
that would allow for sex.

Passionate elements of foreplay
once indulged by lovers.
Uninhibited acts of intercourse—
the stimulation to a relationship.

Routine acts of expectation
cause a predictable breakup.
Yet amicable understanding
offers a promise of friendship.

Circumstances of intimate proximity
must by handled with restraint,
avoiding all advances
in an effort to maintain balance.

Fragile human emotions
strain underlying wants.
Conflict of overwhelming elements
emphasizes the power of temptation.

THE PLAY

Undocumented reasoning
behind one of life's
greatest moments.

Struggling to achieve
an elusive goal.

Trapped within loneliness,
opportunity appears
a distance away.

Yesterday's imperfections
complicate satisfaction
in a delicate affair.

Swirling about
in a sea of humanity,
pulled helplessly below.

Wondering if ever
the aguish will subside.

Questioning the doubt
that lingers within.

Amid millions,
a singularity that
hopes to multiply.

Emotionally vulnerable
to the complicated
rituals of romance.

Mimicking the dance
of human seduction.

COURTSHIP RITUALS

Lone individuals rehearsing scenes:
    conversion,
    dance,
    work,
    and leisure activity.
Desired companionship
necessitates varying approaches:
    notes,
    classifieds,
    suggestive touch,
    and direct approach.
Eventual result
fluctuates in degrees:
    ignorance,
    misunderstanding,
    embarrassment,
    and rejection.

Without,
furthers the sense of isolation.

Overlooked,
misery is further increased.

Forsaken,
one's descent only increases.

Alone,
confined to eternal solitary.

Imposed reflection
gradually leads to improvement.

Dissecting failure
can allow for change.

Broadened perspective
recognizes its own rewards.

Self-worth is best established from within.

HANDS OVER HEART

Emotionally struggling
to find overall purpose.
A personal journey
complicated by truth.

Hands over heart,
striving to be complete.

Clinging to others
while plunging deep.
Searching for answers
where little exists.

Distractions mislead
from the ultimate focus.
Searching for beliefs
that have no foundation.

Hands reaching out
for someone to hold.

Heart skips a beat
as desperation grows.

Wandering about
without any pattern,
despite opinions
from so many others.

Intimate strangers
cautiously hold hands.

Vulnerable loners
exposing one's heart.

Temporary treasures
feed unnecessary thoughts.
A challenging scenario
without any clues.

Minimizing dangers
while sacrificing love.
Occupying the shadows,
avoiding the benefits of light.

Hands over heart
stimulate a rhythm
to an orchestrated beat.

LOVE IS...

Human embodiment
of absolute contentment,
composed of emotions
derived from the heart
rather than rational thoughts
from the head.

No greater bond
ever could exist
between mother and child.

Neither lust nor perversion,
but a commitment of trust
and absolute understanding
between two beings.

An elusive state
compounded by sacrifice.

Love.

Many have I hurt,
searching for a connection.

Opposite of hatred and anger,
built upon a foundation
of mutual respect
within a relationship.

Blinded by arousal,
I have relentlessly pursued
short-term satisfaction.

Fundamental necessity
toward an everlasting connection.
Comprised of sensitivity,
woven from vulnerability
instead of violent reactions.
Love heals all.

THE JOURNEY

Hand in hand,
the journey begins.
An infinite unknown
of limited success.
Idealists within a dream
worshiping the fairytale.
Amateurs at courtship
tutored by rituals.
Commitment and understanding
strengthens the bond.

Side by side,
an excursion is planned.
With greater clarity,
the foundation is build.
Lovers without distraction,
declaring a relationship.
Adults take on responsibility
in each gradual step.
Caring and concern
establishes stability.

Heart to heart,
linked by synchronicity.
Coupled in focus,
a future is solidified.
Partners fully orientated
to each other's expectations.

Elders gain wisdom
passed along to generations.
Sympathy and compassion
reinforces promises.

One
and another,
collectively as two.

Marriage

Love
complicated by faith
and societal
complication.

Customs and ceremonies
overwhelm
innocent souls.

Promises
further reinforced
by vows
Of the heart.

Institutions and witnesses
solidify
a legal union.

Bonds
made everlasting
with rings
exchanged between two.

Doubts and questions
threaten
future security.

MY BALKAN BEAUTY

Personified with traditions
quite diverse from my own,
a strong-willed individual
devoted to ideals of the past.

You are my Balkan beauty,
unique in every way.

Rich with features
defined by a culture
and a history
among the Albanian people.

My Balkan beauty
to whom none can compare.

The spell you cast
upon this heart
is both exotic
and unusually mystifying.

An expressive being
whose knowledge is vast.
Instilled with wisdom
and consideration toward others.

The only person able
to ensnare my heart.

A refined Balkan beauty
merged with a boony person.

My lifetime partner,
steadfast in her commitment
and unwavering passion,
nurtures my maturity.

Our matrimonial union,
although often tested,
remains forever steadfast.

APPLE CHEEKS

Rosy red,
sweet and succulent—
my adorable, feisty bride.
An old-fashioned romantic
who's passionately devoted
to her unsophisticated man.

Natural beauty,
radiant and remarkable.

I'm one lucky Neanderthal
to have harvested
the ultimate fruit.
A mixture of tart
and limitless tang,
she nourishes my appetite.

Often guilty
of underappreciation.

Her many qualities
I have never
fully reimbursed.
Know this:
my apple cheeks
fulfil my desire.

TRUST

Love and tenderness
creates a bond.

Commitments between two
strengthens the resolve.

Honour and respect
solidify the union.

Togetherness into one
defines the future.

Doubts and questions
reveal past digressions.

Mysteries appear
out of nowhere.

Petty arguments
lead to separation.

Apart,
desire for each other
grows.

Closeness,
physical and emotional
stability.

Present,
days promise unknown
future.

Required evidence
builds upon assurance.

Loyalty and honesty
bring about trust.

CONFLICT AND CONVERSATION

Opposite attraction
develops beyond
a physical engagement
into a long-term relationship.

Temporary courting rituals
increasingly become scarce.

Verbal aggression
overwhelms the situation.
Enraged emotions
cause momentary blindness.

Stubborn silence
infuriates a ceasefire.
Bottled-up feelings
wedge couples apart.

Apologies are forthcoming
without any lasting resolution.

Understanding never happens
to bridge the growing gap.

Conflict unleashes
verbal hostility
toward unresolved hurt.

Mutual conversation
initiates the healing
and eventual respect.

Openness and honesty
breaks down the walls.

Unflinching clarity
can focus the illusion.

Despite the difficulties,
love is worth the fight.
Awareness of one another
helps fortify the bond.

Determination is the key
to a lengthy solution.
Unyielding commitment
will ensure success.

Worthy characteristics
magnify the passion.

Enlightened personalities
fuse two distinct minds.
What was once physical
flourishes into promise.

LEFT BEHIND

One
moves on,
while another's
left behind.

Lengthy relationships—
an insurmountable
challenge.

Abandoned
from security,
loved ones
left totally alone.

Spontaneous lovers—
a volatile
circumstance.

Betrayal
and deceit
ruthlessly victimize
the innocent.

Substitute parent
overwhelmed by
responsibilities.

Lost,
wandering endlessly,
searching for
the truth.

Routine behaviour
void of any
expectations.

Confused
by questions
that have
no certain answers.
Conflicting emotions
build momentum
behind suffering.

Regret
from mistakes
that have no
logical explanation.

Left behind,
helpless to the
elements.

MORTALITY

Brief moments begin
a journey toward uncertainty.
Mobility and abilities—
testaments of purpose.

Bodies of fragile dependence
striving to achieve independence.
Time acts upon its bargain,
seizing its advantage.

Countless battles waged,
though victory may be futile.
Life becomes cumbersome
with death lurking nearby.

Struggling against the unknown
despite an outcome predetermined.

BATTLING BACK

Sudden illness
cripples an active lifestyle.
Harrowing challenges
mean a lengthy recovery.

Shadowed by loneliness
despite the company of family.

Subjected to testing
with unforeseen consequence.
Medical professionals
gamble with your health.

Permanent scarring
emphasize a courageous battle.
Poisonous medications
add to the consequences.

Depression and weakness
complicate your emotional state.

Minor details
become greatly diminished.

Daily survival
tampered by surrender
burdens an innocent life.
Words of encouragement
spark renewed hope.

Reflection and meaning
necessitate a means to fight.

Precious moments
fulfil a greater cause.

Promising results
illuminate a second chance.
Technological advances
bring about better odds.
Rejuvenated organs
minimize earlier damage.
Promising prognosis
helps in the road to recovery.

Spiritually enlightened
by loved ones.

Overcoming severity
allows a new sense of worth.
Ability and insight
instil upon a few.

PASSING

Upon these fertile waters,
we cast your ashes
this day.

A father,
a son,
a brother,
and a devoted husband

May you find peace
and tranquillity
in life's final journey.

Within nature's
greatest symphony,
each wave and ripple
calms the pain.

Though no longer
among us,
your memories will last.

A child,
a man,
a mentor,
and someone special.

One day we
will join you.
Once more our family
will then be complete.

Till then,
we say good-bye,
as your spirit is set free.

IMMORTALITY

Life begins
as a chance.
Vast opportunities
with a clean slate.

Infinite possibilities
confined solely by environment.

Child's play
oblivious to reality.
Learned student
relying upon elders' guidance.

Unforeseen burdens
dictated by society.

Teenage recklessness
endanger a promising future.
Vulnerable adolescent
hampered by increasing responsibilities.

Financial necessity
forces academic abandonment.

Experience
and wisdom
rarely come
without a price.

Memories
shared among others
grant one
spiritual immortality.

ABOUT THE AUTHOR

Kenneth W. Westdorp is a student of human emotions, seeking to be both open-minded and wise as to their delicate balance. His diverse poetic style captures the mood and stark reality of the human existence. He lives with his wife, Ardita, in Surrey, British Columbia, Canada.

Printed and bound by PG in the USA